This book belo

STRIVING FOR A GREENER FUTURE

Written by: Sustain
Printed by: Tewkesbury Printing
Illustrated by: Alex Crump

FACT!
8 out of every 10 species found on land live in forests.

It's Friday morning in the wood,
And creatures gather, brave and good.
Let me introduce you to,
The members of the Ecocrew:

Sue the squirrel and wise owl Ollie,
Fred the fox and hedgehog Harry.

With a *flutter* and a *tweet,*
Ollie owl began to speak...

"Listen, listen everyone,
Before our forest is overrun,
It's time for you to learn some more,
About our home and what it's for,
The quest will be to collect some leaves,
But listen closely to the trees."

"Come on Sue, don't fall behind,
We'll lose you as the path unwinds!"
"I'm catching up now, sorry Fred,
You know that you have bigger legs!"
"Look you guys, just up ahead,
I see an *Oak tree*," Harry said...

Soon the friends could see a stream,
In the sun, they watched it gleam....

"I am Willow, *soft* and *gentle*
But my bark is quite essential,

It helps the doctors make you better
When you feel under the weather,

So keep me safe and you can take,
My Willow leaf, from the lake."

FACT!
Willow tree bark is used to make medicines.

Another turn and they could see,
What looked just like a *Christmas tree*...

"Hello friends my name is Pine,
Look how tall my branches climb,
My wood grows back so very fast,
Use me for your *books* and *cards*,
Make sure you paper is FSC,
Now you can have a gift from me."

FACT! The FSC symbol tells you that paper is eco-friendly.

"My name is Ash and here I stand,
My branches are so **tall** and **grand**.
Now take a leaf, go on your way,
Or else I fear I'll talk all day.
But careful Sue, it's getting dark,
Don't stray too far from the path."

FACT!
Some ash trees are 80 feet tall... that's more than 10 buses piled on top of each other!

"Help us please!" The creatures blared,
And just like magic, in the air,
Ollie Owl would guide them back,
He flew above the woodland track.
Safe at last they understood,
Just what was ruining their wood.

"Well children what a day you've had,
The things you've seen are very sad,
But now you know about the trees,
Can you present me with your leaves?"
One by one the friends laid down,
Their hard earned prizes on the ground...

"We've learnt so much about the trees,
We find it quite hard to believe,
How anyone could burn them down,"
Said Harry with a thoughtful frown.

It's time to have your own adventure!

Get outside and get creative to earn your Ecobadge...

Dear Ecowarrior,

This is what you need to do to earn your Ecobadge...

- Complete your Ecodiary ◼
- Make your own bug hotel ◼
- Colour in some wildlife pictures ◼
- Have a go at our woodland puzzle page ◼
- Make your own chocolate bird nests ◼
- Complete our outdoor adventure ◼
- Play some of our games outside ◼

Tick them off as you complete them. Good luck!

From, The Ecocrew

My Ecodiary

Eco Warrior Name:

Draw your favorite animal in here:

Write about your favorite wildlife experience here:
_____
_____
_____
_____
_____
_____
_____
_____
_____

Draw your favorite tree here:

Help Sue and the Ecocrew Build a Bugs Hotel

You will need:
A large plastic bottle
Leaves
Twigs
Soil

You could also add:
Pinecones
Straw
Bark

1. Carefully cut the top and bottom off the plastic bottle so you are left with a tube. This will be the support holding the hotel together.

2. Collect some different types and sizes of leaves and lay them out, ready to put in your hotel. You can add some hay and bark here too.

4. Fill your hotel with soil to act as the base of the hotel. Insects live in damp areas so you could also add a sprinkle of water too!

5. Add all of your materials into your hotel, making sure the twigs are held tightly together. Its great to add anything natural that you find outside at this stage. Not only leaves, twigs and hay but a few pebbles will provide a perfect home for creepy crawlies!

6. Add other leaves on top and all around to help it blend in with the environment. We don't want to scare the small bugs! Small insects also spend a lot of time in the dark so this will be perfect for them.

7. Then you are ready to place your brand new hotel in your garden ready for bugs to explore! Make sure you keep this in your garden as we don't want anyone else accidentally breaking it.

Scan this code to see our team making the Bugs hotel:

Help the crew colour these woodland plants and flowers

Fun and Games!

How many words can you find?

E	L	W	N	T	R	A	B	B	I	T	Z
S	F	A	G	H	E	D	G	E	H	O	G
A	O	L	H	S	E	V	C	J	K	I	U
F	C	O	W	L	P	B	N	R	A	K	M
S	P	S	I	Y	T	O	A	E	L	J	O
U	G	X	L	B	I	A	H	C	E	M	I
S	A	Z	L	I	N	K	B	Y	A	L	C
T	S	C	O	R	Y	L	K	C	V	P	P
A	H	P	W	C	F	O	X	L	E	A	I
I	R	B	A	H	A	K	H	E	S	C	N
N	J	O	L	E	G	O	R	E	C	T	E
R	F	S	A	B	T	F	M	A	B	U	Q

HEDGEHOG, SUSTAIN, OAK, BIRCH, RECYCLE, WILLOW, RABBIT, ASH, OWL, FOX, PINE, LEAVES

Did you know?
The worlds smallest species of snail is 1mm in height! So, it can fit through the eye of a needle.

Oh no! Sue has lost her badge. Can you her help find it in the maze?

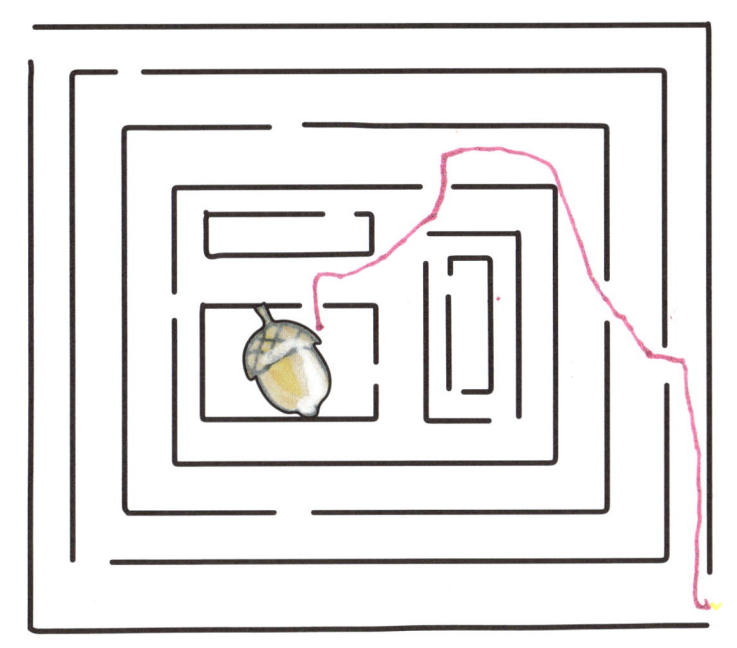

Can you match the paw print to each member of the crew?

Sue   Harry   Fred   Ollie

Make your own Chocolate Bird Nests!

Birds make homes high in the trees! Earn your Ecobadge by making some tasty chocolate bird nests.

You will need:

200g of milk chocolate
85g of crushed wheat cereal
2 tablespoons of golden syrup

Equiment:

Cupcake cases
A bowl
A saucepan
A cupcake tray

1. Break the chocolate into pieces and place in a large bowl.

2. Place the bowl over a pan of near-boiling water and melt, making sure to stir it regularly. Be very careful with the hot pan and bowl and ensure you have an adult to help you.

3. Add in the crushed wheat cereal and stir well to combine the ingredients. Birds go exploring to find all of the twigs to put in their nests, they do this to make it a nice and strong home!

4. Add two tablespoons of golden syrup to the mixture and continue to stir.

5. Place 12 cupcake cases on a tray. It's best to use a cupcake tray if you have one.

6. Using a spoon place the chocolate wheat mixture into different cupcake cases.

7. Press a teaspoon into the chocolate wheat mixture, forming a nest shape.

8. Add your own decorations and leave the nests to set in the fridge for 2 hours.

Scan this code to see our team making the Chocolate bird nests:

Complete our outdoor adventure!

Ask an adult to take you out and about and see if you can spot some of these things...

A duck = 2 points

A snail = 1 point

A butterfly = 3 points

A flower = 2 points

A spider or spiders web = 2 points

A mouse = 3 points

How many points did you get?

Outside Games!

Try playing our outdoor noughts and crosses game.

Hunt on the ground for some sticks to use for the board. Then collect some rocks or pebbles to use as markers. Lay them out on the ground to play with your friends and family outside.

Play pooh sticks with a friend. Choose your sticks from the ground and drop them from a bridge into a stream at the same time. See who's reaches the other side of the bridge first!

Visit our website by scanning this code to access lots more fun activities:
Or use: https://www.sustainye.com
Happy reading!